ADJUSTING AND REPAIRING Violins, 'Cellos, &c.

A Practical Handbook for all Players

BY
ARTHUR BROADLEY

ILLUSTRATED

LONDON

1923

MADE AND PRINTED IN GREAT BRITAIN
BY JARROLD AND SONS, LTD., NORWICH

PUBLISHER'S PREFACE

THE interest and enthusiasm which the articles on "Violin Repairing" excited during their serial run in *The Bazaar* fully warrant the appearance of the present little manual; and we must acknowledge our indebtedness to several correspondents who have greatly assisted by their queries. To be of the greatest service is not always "to tell all one knows," but "to tell that which others require to know."

If the healing art is the divine art, surely some virtue attaches to the repairing of violins Who will repay one for the hours, perhaps days, or even months of labour that may be required to restore the wheezy old derelict into a sweet singer? It would be a good thing if all violins were perfect, not requiring adjustment or repair, but as that is not possible in this world of "falls and bruises," the next best thing is to know how to repair scientifically and artistically. We trust that all our readers will find something in the ensuing pages which will be of interest and of use in attaining that end.

Adjusting and Repairing Violins, 'cellos, &c.

CHAPTER I.

INTRODUCTION.

DURING my professional career it has been forced upon me that not one per cent. of violins, violoncellos, &c., are fitted in such a manner that justice is done to their tonal powers. I have on several occasions had the good luck to change the character of tone of an instrument completely, and so to improve it that its former owner could scarcely believe his own ears. In the following chapters I shall endeavour to instruct the amateur player and the collector how to make the most of their treasures, both from a tonal and from an artistic point of view.

With the exception of a few good firms—and a smaller number of "private makers"—the repairing and restoration of violins have been entirely neglected. It is essential that a maker or repairer should be able in some degree to play the instrument; he must also know something of the technique of advanced playing. Lack of this knowledge is answerable for much of the trashy work turned out by "shops"—establishments where the knowledge of pianos, organs, and the sheet-music trade is pre-eminent—and is also responsible for the unplayable condition in which many of the "warehouse" violins seem to be. Some of my pupils and professional friends have said: "It is not that So-and-so do not know how to fit up an instrument nicely: it is because they do not care to trouble about adjusting any instrument which is not bought at their establishment." Be this as it may, I will give some hints how to convert a common warehouse fiddle, viola, or 'cello into a playable instrument, or a toneless, broken, resin-covered, filthy old specimen into a "thing of beauty and a joy for ever."

Tools.

Although almost every maker has his own special tools and devices, nothing of an extraordinary nature is needed. An ordinary joiner's bench with a wooden screw-vice is a luxury. A

Introduction. 3

good kitchen table with an iron clamp-vice will do quite as well. The usual array of carpenters' small tools, such as a brace and bits, a smoothing-plane, various sizes of chisels, a fretsaw, palette-knife, &c., are the chief implements. Add to these a pair of callipers and several bent and bevelled gouges as used by wood-carvers, small screw-clamps—both of wood and the iron ones, as used by fret-workers—and you have all but the special tools. The latter include a bending-iron, both for bending the ribs and for purfling; a purfling tool, which in reality is only a "double-marker"; and several small iron planes, one or two of which must have the cutting-tool well up to the front. I have seen many violins which were made with the usual joiner's and wood-carver's tools. Messrs. Haynes and Co., Ltd., of 122, King's Cross Road, W.C. 1, supply everything necessary for making and repairing violins and 'cellos; and from Mr. George Buck, of 242, Tottenham Court Road, W., all the required tools may be obtained.

CHAPTER II.

ADJUSTING A 'CELLO.

THE first instrument to which I will devote my energies is an ordinary warehouse 'cello. It was purchased from a well-known London firm by one of my pupils for a sum sufficiently high to demand attention. The tone on the bass strings is something like that which would be produced by a matchbox, while the A string is shrill and squeaking.

The first thing that my pupil complains of is "that his 'cello is not so easy to play on as mine." On examining the bridge this is at once apparent; the bridge is so high that the strings are quite an inch away from the finger-board. It is difficult to stop the notes which are in the lower neck positions, and quite impossible to play on the D and G strings in the higher positions, as the bow touches the A and C. From the appearance of the instrument it is quite evident that until my pupil bought it, a bow had never been drawn across the strings. The bridge had been "put up," and that is all that can be said to have been done in the way of adjustment.

Trimming and Fitting the Bridge.

First of all I make an attempt to fit the feet of the bridge to the table of the 'cello. This is of far greater importance than is at first apparent. I take a sharp-pointed instrument (the steel point of a pair of compasses does well), and holding the bridge upright, I follow the curve of the belly, and describe a similar curve with the point of the compasses. This can be done with a lead pencil; the only disadvantage is that where a sharp steel point makes one fine, clear-cut line, the point of a pencil—no matter how sharp it may be—makes a jagged, blurred line. I now cut away the wood with a sharp penknife.

A delicate matter is to get the under surface of the foot quite in touch with the surface of the belly, or upper table, of the 'cello. In order to accomplish this I adopt the following plan :

Slightly wetting the surface of the wood, I

scrape away the foot until, if anything, it is slightly hollow; then I take a piece of medium glass-paper and lay the rough side upwards exactly on the spot where the bridge will stand. Gripping the bridge firmly, and taking care to hold it quite perpendicularly—or if anything leaning a shade towards the tail-piece—I move the bridge slightly upwards and downwards. In doing this I move not more than half the width of the feet away, either upwards or downwards. The result is, or should be, a perfect fit.

I now proceed to cut away the top of the bridge; the A string I fit to $\frac{1}{2}$in. from the finger-board at its extreme end, the D and G almost $\frac{3}{8}$in., and the C according to the shape of the finger-board. In this case the board is very much cut away, so I only allow about $\frac{1}{4}$in.

The above measurements are well on the fine side; for orchestral playing I should make the strings a very little higher. It is seldom that a 'cello requires the strings at a greater distance than $\frac{3}{8}$in. from the board—that is, in these days of rapid technique in the higher positions.

Having got the desired curve (as indicated in Fig. 1), I now make some attempt to trim the bridge. On looking at the bridge which I have taken off the 'cello I find that it is almost

Adjusting a 'cello. 7

exactly of the same shape and thickness as when it was purchased (as indicated in the dotted outlines in Figs. 1 and 2). That must be altered. Drawing a line down the centre of the upper edge of the bridge, and also down the centre of each edge, I use these marks as

Fig. 1. Front View of 'Cello Bridge, showing how the legs and sides should be trimmed. The dotted lines indicate an ill-fitting bridge.

a guide and carefully cut away the wood until it tapers to a little over $\frac{1}{16}$in. at the extreme top. This tapering is done evenly, not as in the dotted line in Fig. 2. I also cut away the superfluous wood on the legs and feet of the bridge, and trim and slightly bevel the outside edges (Fig. 1). It will be seen that the finished shape of the bridge is very different from that which was previously fitted to the 'cello.

On trying the 'cello, I find a vast improvement on the lower strings; but the A string is yet

Fig. 2. Side View of 'Cello Bridge. The tapering should be gradual, and not as indicated by the dotted lines.

hard and squeaky, while on the G string is one of those horrid sounds termed a "wolf note." The bridge is as perfect as it can be, so I must now look at that most important accessory the sound-post.

Adjusting a 'cello.

Fitting the Sound-post.

Slackening the strings until all pressure is taken off the bridge, and it barely stands, I then see whereabouts the post is fixed. As I thought, it is too near the foot of the bridge—almost under it! No wonder the A string is tense and harsh in its sound; no wonder the lower strings sound as if their tone were produced from a matchbox! My sound-post setter is a curved steel instrument, sharpened to a point at one end, and at the other fitted with a sort of prongs. Inserting the setter, I try to move the post. In nine cases out of ten it would, if properly fitted, immediately fall. But no; it neither moves nor falls. It is, in fact, so jammed that it takes the utmost force to move it, and then it falls with a bang.

Having supplied myself with a little mirror with a long, bent handle, I insert this, and examine the place where the post has pushed against the upper table. Once again the cheap maker has erred grievously. He has not made any attempt to bevel the top of the post to the curve of the upper table. The result is that one sharp edge of the post has quite embedded itself in the soft pine, leaving a nasty dent. I take a little off the top of the post, making it somewhat sloping, so that when it is again inserted the top and bottom exactly fit the curves of the upper and lower tables. While manipulating the post I apply a little pressure to the upper table, relieving this pressure when wishing to move the post, and applying it when I think it is at last in position. I pull out the sharpened point of the setter, and tighten up the strings, keeping an eye on the bridge to see that it is quite perpendicular.

The sound-post should fit "easily." That is to say, it should exert just as much pressure on the upper and lower tables as will keep it in place when the pressure of the strings is taken off.

At last the 'cello is properly adjusted. I have placed the sound-post about $\frac{1}{2}$in. behind the left foot of the bridge, and if anything slightly nearer the centre of the 'cello. This gives the best tone on all the four strings. The A string is now beautiful and round, and has sufficient brilliance; the D and G are vastly improved, and now that I have put on a thinner G string I find the "wolf" has quite gone. The C has lost much of its hollow tone, and for a 'cello of this description is very good. My pupil is astonished at the transformation in the tone and appearance of his 'cello, and he can play on it in every position with great facility.

CHAPTER III.

RESTORING AN OLD VIOLIN.

THE next instrument to which I will direct attention is an old English violin. It is one of those instruments which have been cherished in the family for generations. Each generation has added its mark. So varied and so interesting are these marks, and so useful for my purpose, that I give a sketch of the upper table in all its glory (Fig. 3). Two huge fractures disfigure the treble side of the belly; one runs from the upper bout to the sound-hole, the other from the lower part of the sound-hole to the lower bout. The upper corner on the same side has been jagged off, and is still missing; the lower corner has been inartistically repaired by the insertion of a piece of polished mahogany. The repairer had evidently a true eye for colour! After he had skilfully inserted the mahogany patch, with the grain running at cross-angles to the grain of the belly, he found that it was rather too red in shade, and so to add to his sins he actually *painted* that portion of the belly adjoining the patch a deep red. Another member

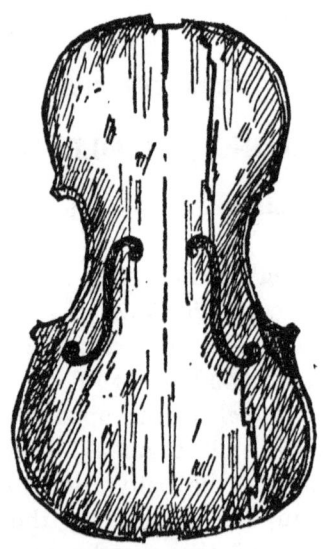

Fig. 3. Outer Surface of Upper Table of Violin, showing extent and nature of fractures.

of the family—evidently in the boot-repairing trade—has skilfully introduced a reminiscence of his craft in the shape of a piece of cobblers' wax, to fill up a fracture at the lower left bout.

Restoring an Old Violin. 13

Cleaning.

First of all, I will clean and string up the violin to see if the tone is all right. If this is fairly good, the fractures must, if possible, be repaired without taking off the upper table. To remove the sticky red paint I try, first of all, a little Eau-de-Cologne. Here I must caution my readers regarding the use of spirits in any form for cleaning an instrument. The slightest drop of Eau-de-Cologne on the varnish will sometimes soften it and cause it to come off.

I have, however, a severe case to deal with, and must adopt drastic measures. The Eau-de-Cologne certainly touches the paint, but does not remove it rapidly enough. I therefore provide myself with some good ammonia and a cotton rag. In using the Eau-de-Cologne, and also the ammonia, I am careful that none of the liquid *drops* on the varnish. The paint rapidly dissolves, and comes away on the rag. I repeatedly change the rag, and on getting down to the varnish I use greater care.

Removing Superfluous Glue.

After trying the tone, I find that the G string is very weak, and on looking through the sound-hole observe that the bar is the original one;

so the table must come off to have a new bar fitted, and this without causing any further fractures. After removing the strings, tailpiece, &c., I carefully look along the joining of the table and ribs to see if I can find a place where the table has sprung at all. The last "repairer" has, however, quite anticipated this catastrophe, and has plastered a thick, dark substance—intended for glue—inside and out.

I must now get rid of this superfluous glue. It is of so brittle a nature, and adheres so to the varnish, that to attempt to force off the table would be to court disaster. I take a cup of hot water and an old tooth-brush, and carefully scrub away at the glue, now and again wiping away the water and the softened glue with a cotton rag. My patience is eventually rewarded; the presence of so much glue outside the work told me that the joint would be neither close nor firmly fixed.

Removing the Upper Table, or Belly.

As soon as the thick glue is wiped away I find that the table springs away in several places. Inserting the thin, flat blade of an old table knife into one of the gaping joints, and carefully regulating its progress by applying pressure with my left hand where needed, I

Restoring an Old Violin. 15

gradually work the knife all the way round, using care when the upper and lower blocks are reached, also at the corners, and still greater care where the fractures make their appearance.

At last the upper table comes away. It is lucky that I decided to take off the table, for I find that its previous owner—or some jack-knife joiner—has plastered up the inside of the belly with cotton rag well soaked with glue—certainly a primitive way of repairing a fracture.

It is often possible to repair a newly-made fracture, either in the upper table or in the ribs, without taking off the belly. An ingenious way of doing this, which I have never seen or heard of anyone but myself attempting, I will describe later.

It often happens in the case of old instruments which one picks up that the insides get completely covered with studs, inserted by first one repairer, then another. In these cases a good job can be made only by opening the violin. The presence of a number of small pieces of wood in the interior and much thick glue completely smothers the tone. Once more I take my old tooth-brush and hot water, and soak and brush away until the cotton rags come away and also the superfluous glue.

Removing the Bass-Bar.

As I proceed with this work I occasionally let some hot water soak on the bass bar; in fact, I place along its whole length a cotton rag soaked in hot water. By the time I have removed the cotton plasters and the thick glue with which they have been spread, and nicely cleaned the place, I find the bass-bar almost ready to come away. Taking a thin, flexible palette-knife, I insert the tip between the bass-bar and the belly, and so well has the hot water done its work that the bar springs away; another wipe is given with the wet rag, and the upper table is then ready for treatment.

Now, few repairers—and my experience of them has been considerable—would be content to wait until the glue which affixed the bar to the upper table was softened by the application of hot water, but with a chisel or gouge would in a few strokes split and rip off the bar. In nine cases out of ten the result would be that the belly would be splintered. Glue that has hardened requires careful treatment; anyone who has attempted to break up an ordinary cake of glue knows that it splits and flies about in a most wonderful fashion. So it is if drastic measures are attempted in removing it from the surface or the inner parts of violins. Before the

Restoring an Old Violin. 17

glue will separate it will chip off the varnish, or, if inside the instrument, it will bring off with it splinters of the wood.

Repairing the Upper Table.

I now make preparations to restore the belly to its original condition. I have by me a piece of sycamore board, perfectly level and true on both its surfaces, and about a couple of inches thick. To all intents and purposes it is as true and solid as a block of marble; its shape is an oblong slightly larger than the table of a violin. This I use in much the same way as an entomologist employs his mounting-board.

Taking the table—which is now in two portions—I lay it on the board and proceed so to "pad" it that it assumes its original shape. Unless the original curves which the belly had before it was fractured can again be produced, it will be impossible to repair the cracks with anything like neatness.

The pad which I build up on the sycamore slab is composed of anything handy—a piece or two of thin pine, some veneer, and, lastly, several layers of brown paper and blotting-paper; this pad I fasten with drawing-pins to the slab. On again placing the belly—outside upwards of course—on the slab, I find that when the edges touch the slab—which I of course leave clear and free the whole way round—the belly assumes its natural curve, and by the slightest pressure the cracks so meet that scarcely a join is visible. Having by means of two or three small screw-clamps fastened the edges of the belly to the sycamore slab, thus assuring me that the edges will be perfectly true when the job is finished, I quickly run in some glue, and, pressing the edges closely together, wipe away any glue which oozes out.

I now wind some string around the slab and the belly, and as string is inclined to "give," I observe minutely the fracture to see if, as the glue sets, it has sprung at all. As a safeguard I insert small pads of blotting-paper under the string. This answers a double purpose: it wedges the fractured edges closer together, and also keeps the string away from any superfluous glue. The work must not again be touched until the glue has properly hardened; indeed, it is advisable to leave it for a night. When the glue has properly set I clean the mended portion with a little warm water.

Repairing the Corners of the Upper Table.

Now I proceed to repair the corners. Dispensing with the piece of mahogany which has

Restoring an Old Violin.

been attached, and taking a very sharp paring chisel, I cut a clean, sharp edge in that portion of the fractured belly where a corner has to be joined. I have by me several bits of old pine; some of it is part of the sounding-board of an old piano, and this I find matches the grain or thread of the violin belly to a nicety. I cut a piece of this slightly larger and also somewhat thicker than is required. Some little patience is needed to fit the grain of the pine thread to thread, but at last I am successful.

The corner is now treated in a similar way to the fracture in the belly, only in this case we have two true edges to meet, and not two fractured edges. The upper corner and the missing piece at the lower portion of the belly I treat in a similar manner, in each case making the edges of the broken belly quite true without cutting away too much wood, and also leaving in each instance the new piece somewhat thicker than is required. The under-side of the repairs I keep perfectly flat and true; the superfluous thickness protrudes above the surface of the belly.

The new pine inserted being still in the rough, and slightly thicker than is required, I take a sharp gouge and very carefully pare away the wood until the curves are identical with the remaining portions of the work. The purfling I insert at this stage (as described in a later chapter), and once more clean the work.

Affixing Studs.

Some small studs of pine not thicker than a penny in their stoutest part, and about the size

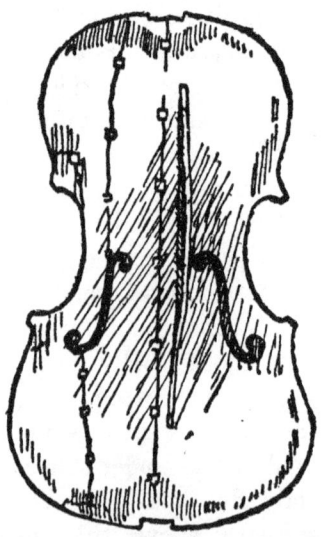

Fig. 4. Inner Surface of Upper Table of Violin, showing bass-bar and method of strengthening cracks by the addition of studs.

of a threepenny-piece, are now prepared. These are glued at distances of, say, 1½in. along the inside of the belly (as in Fig. 4), and the edges

Restoring an Old Violin.

of the fracture carefully bound together. I take care that the grain of the studs goes *across* the fracture, not *with* it.

The further work on the instrument under repair will be dealt with in succeeding chapters.

CHAPTER IV.

INSERTING A NEW BASS-BAR, &c.

I NOW arrive at a most important matter—the bass-bar. The new bass-bar I have already cut from a strip of fine old pine; it is a trifle longer than the old one, which has been removed, and is tapering in shape (as in Fig. 4), and nicely bevelled and finished off. A roughly-made bass-bar is responsible for much faulty tone.

I am now at a portion of the subject which requires some consideration. The position of the bass-bar has been much discussed; one maker puts it parallel with the centre joining of the belly : another causes it to incline inwards at its upper end to a greater or lesser degree. Experience has proved to me that the build of an instrument and its inherent faults govern the position, the length, the depth, and the thickness of the bar.

In order to show the utter ignorance which

many repairers display on the subject, I will here mention an incident which will also serve to throw a little light on this somewhat intricate matter. I took an old instrument to be repaired, and at the same time asked if anything could be done to give more tone in the bass string. "Oh," said the repairer, "it requires a new bass-bar; all these old instruments require longer bars." I allowed him to experiment in his own way, and the result was complete disaster. Although the bass string had in some measure gained a sort of "wooden" tone, the whole instrument had suffered considerably. This was an instance where it was unsafe to follow any generally-accepted theory.

On taking off the belly I found that all the known rules had been observed. I now commenced to experiment on my own lines. I took out the offending bar, and inserted one which, although it contained the same weight of wood as the modern bar, was the same length as the old one. I also altered the position of the bar, making it conform more to the angle of the sound-holes, which were in this instance almost perpendicular. The results were an added brilliancy to all the four strings and much greater resonance in the lower part of the register.

24   Adjusting and Repairing Violins, &c.

It is not safe to argue on a single instance, but I may say with some authority that although in most cases old violins in their original state are fitted with bass-bars which are far too weak for modern requirements, the merits of each particular instrument must be studied before it can be stated whether a longer bar will improve the tone or not.

To return to the violin under notice. The bar which I insert is placed almost parallel with the middle joint, as the peculiarity of structure demands—in this instance—that it should be so.

The belly is now ready for gluing on the body of the instrument. Before I do this I remove some of the superfluous studs which an over-anxious maker has placed down the centre joint. Six or eight at the most are ample, where my violin has thirteen. I therefore remove every alternate stud, and I shall be much surprised if by so doing some little brilliance is not added to the tone of the instrument.

Re-fixing the Upper Table.

In order to re-fix the belly to the ribs and back neatly and expeditiously some experience is necessary.

First of all I prepare some six or seven small screw-clamps, and several pads of pasteboard,

Inserting a New Bass-Bar, &c.

cork, blotting-paper, or any substance that will prevent the clamps from injuring the varnish. The clamps I adjust in such a manner that by a single turn of the screw they can be fixed in position. The whole operation is performed near the fire or gas-stove. First I hold the parts to be glued near the stove until they are fairly warm, then I apply the glue rapidly to the four corners and the upper and lower "flats"—that is, that portion of the belly which on the inner surface is flattened to rest on the end blocks. I also quickly apply some glue—not too much—to the corner blocks and the end blocks, then rapidly fix the belly in position, screw up the clamps, wipe away the superfluous glue, and put the violin aside until the glue has hardened.

When I again take the violin in hand I treat the remainder of the gluing as if the belly had merely "sprung off" at the places not glued. I take the thin palette-knife previously mentioned, and, inserting it in the hot glue, run this into the joining. The clamps are applied as before, and the belly is now properly affixed.

Many makers try to perform this operation at one time; but I do not think it is always advisable. It is scarcely possible to affix the table of a 'cello or a double bass at one operation

—although I have seen this done—and it is advisable, especially in cold weather, to treat the violin as one would the larger instruments, and to affix the belly in two distinct operations.

For the above method of fixing the upper table, and also for several other matters of more than usual interest, I am indebted to the late Mr. William Heaton, the violin maker.

The only matters now remaining are to prepare the new wood for varnishing, to varnish the white wood, to insert the sound-post, to adjust the strings, &c.

Preparing New Wood for Varnishing.

A very important matter must now come under consideration—*i.e.*, the manner of preparing the new wood for the varnish. If the varnish is applied direct to the new white wood, the brilliant light under-ground is forced to show through. I have a very valuable 'cello disfigured in this manner; although the varnish is matched to perfection, in some lights the strip of wood that is inserted shines with such brilliance that it takes on a very much lighter shade than the original portions of the work. In my repairs, however, I treat the whole matter as an artist would treat the restoration of an old picture.

Inserting a New Bass-Bar, &c. 27

Colouring and Varnishing.

With respect to varnish, I think any of the well-known makes, such as, for instance, Whitelaw's Violin Varnish, will suit our purpose. It would be easier to use a spirit varnish pure and simple; but the glare of this can never be removed, and the places repaired would therefore be too much in evidence.

The new portions added must be toned down to the older portions of the work. A variety of substances may be used for this purpose—*e.g.*, gamboge, permanganate of potash, &c. I find, however, that I have attained far more success by using the ordinary artists' water-colours; the colouring matter may then be put on in a variety of shades and depths of tint, imitating with a great degree of success the stained and resin-covered surface of the instrument. I apply in this instance a slight wash of brown, and here and there a few dabs of a darker shade; then varnish, and rub down in the usual way. Varnishing will be fully dealt with in a later chapter.

CHAPTER V.

CUTTING AND FITTING A SOUND-POST.

Now I am about to cut and fit a new sound-post, as I find that the old one is far too thick, and also is pierced with quite a number of holes. Here I may give a few hints on the character and use of the sound-post. The one I have taken out of the instrument was so thick that it would not come out of the sound-hole except through the lower round. The result of such a thick post was to deaden the tone—it acted almost as a mute, checking the vibrations and filling up unnecessarily the air-space of the inside of the instrument. The post I make is of such a thickness that it will slip through the centre of the sound-holes exactly at the place marked with the small cross-cuts. It is made of straight-grained old pine, and in inserting it I take care not to mutilate it with the sound-post setter more than I can possibly help.

Cutting and Fitting a Sound-post.

The sound-post performs two distinct functions: It acts as a transmitter of vibrations from the belly to the back, and thus to the air-space. It also acts as a medium for localising the vibrations, and forms what is known as a node, or nodal point (to which I shall refer later on). Its position is therefore of the greatest importance, and, indeed, the whole character of the tone may be altered by moving the post either nearer to or farther from the bridge, from the sound-bar or bass-bar, or from the sound-hole. We have here a variety of methods of improving the different parts of the register. If the tone is weak on the E and A strings, move the post slightly nearer to the sound-hole; if weak on the G and D, move it nearer to the centre of the instrument; and if the whole character of the instrument is dull and weak in tone, move it nearer to the foot of the bridge.

In experimenting with the sound-post I do not take down the bridge, but loosen the strings so that all tension is removed. When I have at last found the most desirable place, I take a piece of wire and carefully measure the exact position; indeed, I may even go to the extent of marking its position on the back with a lead-pencil. I now take down the strings and bridge, keeping a firm grasp on the belly the while, and remove the end-pin. From this point I can see distinctly whether the post fits at its upper and lower ends. In many cases, even if the post is first made to fit, it has to be moved to a different place, and in its altered position it does not properly adhere to the upper and lower tables.

In case any reader may think all this trouble over the sound-post is a nuisance, let me state once for all that half the ills that violins are heir to may be cured by a nice adjustment of the post. I have seen many an instrument turned from a poor, squeaking thing into one of fine mellow tone merely by correct adjustment of sound-post and bridge.

In a later chapter I shall have something further to say regarding the sound-post and its functions.

CHAPTER VI.

REPAIRING THE RIBS.

YEARS ago, before organs were as numerous as they now are, churches and chapels relied on their local musicians—violinists, violoncellists or "single-bass" players, and "contra-bassists" or "ground-bass" players. These musicians, although often men of genius, were seldom men of culture—at any rate, as far as music was concerned.

It has been my lot to come across a good many old violins and 'cellos which have spent most of their existence in a church or a chapel band. In nearly every instance such instruments have been in the most shocking condition, and often mutilated.

I have now in hand a fine old English violoncello, which I propose to put into proper order. It is a fine instrument of the Banks school, and may have been made by any of the Amati copyists—Hill, Smith, Betts, or Kennedy. As it is evidently of middle-class birth, we must endeavour to restore it to proper playing order in something like an artistic manner, and not in the easiest and cheapest way. The neck has been badly mutilated, besides having several fractures, evidently caused by some inexperienced repairer trying to force the finger-board off. It also has several holes and "frets" cut in it; these are, I should say, to give the positions. In passing, I may remark that the notches are not anywhere near any given scale, making one pity the people who had to listen to the notes produced with such assistance. Besides these eyesores, there is an ugly slip of wood let in between the finger-board and the neck. The body of the 'cello is in fairly good condition, with the exception of two very ugly fractures in the lower ribs, and the whole of the inside is thickly coated with the dust and filth of ages.

A careful examination reveals the repairs necessary. They are: A new neck or graft, of course a new finger-board, and mending of the two fractures in the ribs. As the tone of the 'cello is almost all that can be desired, I will in this instance execute the repairs without removing the upper table.

Repairing the Ribs.

Cleaning the Interior.

First I clean the interior; it is useless to expect glue to adhere to dust. I take a handful of barley which I have previously soaked in water until the grains have become soft and swollen. From this I drain the superfluous water, as of course it is not advisable to "swill" the inside. The damp barley I drop in the interior of the violoncello, and shake about in such a manner that it reaches every corner. Clouds of dust emerge, and after emptying out the barley and repeating the process I find that the interior has quite changed colour.

Removing Glue and Cotton-rag.

On the inside of the fractures is the usual plaster of glue and cotton-rag. This is awkward to reach, but I overcome the difficulty by taking a piece of very stout copper wire, which can be easily bent to any required shape and will retain that shape. On the end of this I tie a $\frac{1}{2}$in. "hog's-hair flat," a brush of the style used by artists for oil painting. An application of hot water soon brings off the plaster, and by fastening a piece of rag at the reverse end of the wire and using as a mop, I very soon have the place quite clean and dry.

The Principles of Gluing.

The too liberal application of the glue-brush has made the fractures appear even worse than they are. Glue is a useful but a most curious substance to deal with. It must be understood that when melted glue sets it contracts; a little globule of melted glue is really hollow when set. The same occurs when two surfaces are coated with glue and brought near together. If the surfaces are true, and are clamped tightly together, so that all possibility of air entering as the glue dries is out of the question, the surfaces adhere to each other. If, on the other hand, the surfaces are not brought sufficiently close together the glue adheres to each surface, leaving a space between the two. Our former repairer has solved the difficulty by liberally running the glue inside and out, thus making it quite impossible for the fracture to "heal."

Closing Fractures in the Ribs.

I find that the edges of the fracture can by internal pressure be brought so close together that it is almost impossible to distinguish the crack from outside. I must, therefore, adopt some method of applying this pressure. Taking a fine needle, I thread it with a good length of

Repairing the Ribs.

tough linen thread. Pressing one edge of the fracture, I find there is ample room to introduce the needle, and, allowing plenty of length to my thread and still retaining hold of the same, I manipulate the instrument until the needle swings out of the sound-hole.

Having previously prepared a small button of hard wood—in this instance pine is not suitable—with a small drill I pierce the button and pass the thread through, securing it with a knot in such a manner that it will stand some pressure. My intention will, I think, now be clear to the reader. After gluing the inner side of the button, I drop it in the interior of the 'cello, and by tightly pulling the linen thread the button is brought up to its position inside the fracture.

My next move is to affix a screw-clamp to the edges of the upper and lower tables in such a way that the edges of the crack are squeezed tightly together, as in Fig. 5. This clamp is also useful for another purpose. I secure the linen thread to it in such a manner that the button is held firmly until the glue is set.

If one button is not sufficient to hold together the edges of the fracture, a second is used in the following manner: I take a very fine drill, and, selecting a place in the fracture which will stand it, I carefully drill a hole, through which I insert the needle and linen thread as before; this hole in many cases is scarcely discernible—the glue fills it up, and when this is set I take an exceedingly sharp knife and cut the thread away quite close.

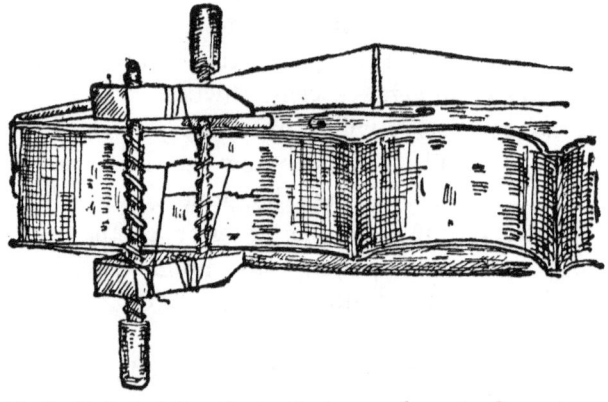

Fig. 5. Method of Clamping-up Fractures and securing Pressure on Studs in the Interior by means of tough Linen Threads.

I find that the 'cello requires three such buttons, and, now that the operation has been successfully carried through, I can say with some pride that the fracture is scarcely visible.

Many repairers would carp at the idea of drilling a fine hole through the ribs, as they would deem such a plan inartistic, but in its place they would load the interior with buttons

Repairing the Ribs.

of pine thickly coated with glue, and, because it is not seen, this is, I suppose, considered allowable. I must again caution the reader against the practice of loading the interior of any instrument with these studs or buttons. They tend to lessen the air space, and act as a mute, clogging the vibrations.

With practice, it is possible to insert two or three studs at one and the same operation. All that is necessary is to prepare the requisite number of threads and to pull all the buttons in place and properly glue them (as explained) at the time of closing the fracture.

It is often possible to close a new fracture without the addition of studs. In such a case the edges must meet so perfectly that the glue which is run between them suffices, and the repair is scarcely visible.

I will now mention another method of inserting a stud. I take a piece of iron wire of the kind that, although it can be bent to any desired shape, yet has a little spring in it, and cut it to the length required. One end I sharpen and insert in the stud, which I glue and affix in its place with the assistance of the wire. The pressure necessary I obtain by affixing a clamp on the opposite side of the 'cello, and against this clamp I spring the wire, thus holding it in position and also giving the necessary pressure to the button from the inside.

Every case has to be treated according to its particular requirements, and the most successful repairer is he who does not blindly follow any set rule, but invents methods of repair which will meet each particular case.

The removal of the old neck and the grafting of the new one are dealt with in the next chapter.

CHAPTER VII.

GRAFTING A NEW NECK.

The grafting of the new neck on to the violoncello dealt with in the preceding pages is an operation of sufficient importance to justify devoting a separate chapter to its consideration.

Removing the Old Neck.

First of all I must remove the neck. This I do by making a cut with a saw as near the root as possible, being exceedingly careful not to damage that little projection against which the neck abuts, and which is termed the button, as with connoisseurs it is of much importance, giving great character to the work. I must not be in too great a hurry to get the neck away, or mind if I have to make several cuts through with the saw, getting nearer and nearer the root, until at last I can cut away the remaining fragments with the chisel. In order to save the button from any injury I make a cut with the saw parallel to the button, and at about half an inch distant. I can then work with some freedom.

In doing this class of work it is advisable to use extreme care. In the old days many of the makers considered that glue was not strong enough for their purpose, so they inserted a large screw right through the upper block into the root of the neck. Otto, in "The Violin," seems also to have discovered this. He says: "The neck is simply glued to the body, not fastened with a nail or screw, as in that case it could not be taken off without removing the belly." It is possible, however, to do even this without taking off the belly. I work as much of the wood away as possible, then chip away the remainder with a small chisel. Now about half an inch or more of the screw-nail is visible. I seize this with a pair of pincers and screw the reverse way. In many cases it is possible by alternately screwing and unscrewing the nail so to enlarge the hole that the nail is easily forced through into the interior of the instrument.

Strengthening and Enlarging the Button.

The button on the 'cello under notice being of a somewhat weak and frail character, it will

Grafting a New Neck.

be impossible to have a good "root" to the
new neck if it is tapered down to this button.
I therefore proceed to strengthen and enlarge
it. I cut the edge quite true and clean with a

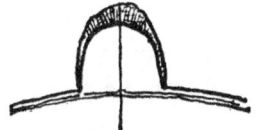

Fig. 6. Badly-shaped Button pared down, the part shaded being cut clear away.

sharp paring chisel (Fig. 6), and then take a
piece of ebony, say, ¼in. thick and somewhat
larger than the button required. On this I
trace the outline of the button with a sharp

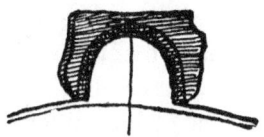

Fig. 7. Method of Attaching Ebony Rim to improve Shape of Button.

steel point, and proceed to glue it in position
(Fig. 7). I roughly cut the ebony away almost
to the traced outline, which I then leave, and
proceed with the new graft.

42 Adjusting and Repairing Violins, &c.

Grafting a New Neck.

The operation of grafting a neck, although one of the most tedious yet mentioned in this little volume, is not beyond the powers of anyone who can use joiners' tools and, more than this, can exercise great care in measuring and finishing off every portion of the work as it proceeds. How often one hears the remark from players of stringed instruments, "Oh! I cannot play this instrument; the neck is so different from the one I am used to." I think violoncellists in particular have reason to grumble, as it is seldom that one comes across even a modern instrument with a nicely-finished neck.

The 'cello at which I am at work is, if anything, slightly smaller than the full-sized Strad. model, but, as it is a fair example of the general build and make of the Old English school, I will give the measurements as they are required for this particular instrument.

Perhaps if I first of all explain what the graft is like it will assist my readers to follow the directions given for its cutting and fitting. The idea of "grafting" a new neck is, of course, to preserve the original scroll—a most important portion of the instrument. The interior of the scroll is so cut away that the end of the new neck is firmly embedded in it, and

Grafting a New Neck. 43

the operation must be so performed that as little as possible of the new wood is seen on the outside. This is accomplished by allowing the outside of the cheeks of the original scroll to remain; the new wood, as it were, lining the interior.

Fig. 8. Side View of Grafted 'Cello Scroll. The dotted lines show the continuation of the grafted new wood in the interior of the peg-box.

Fig. 8 is a side view of the grafted scroll. The dotted lines show the joining of the new wood in the inside of the scroll; the shaded portion shows the original wood. Fig. 9 shows how the graft tapers off—it will be observed that at the most I only cut away half the thickness of the peg-box at its thicker portion, whereas at the upper end the graft tapers quite away. Fig. 10 indicates the shape of the new graft as it emerges from the lower part of the scroll.

Fig. 9. Front View of Grafted 'Cello Scroll. The new wood is shown white.

Setting-out the Neck.

Now to proceed to work. After sawing off the scroll from the original neck, I mark with a sharp-pointed instrument the lines given in Figs. 9 and 10, and, firmly fixing the scroll in a vice, proceed, first with the help of a fine-toothed saw, and afterwards with a keen-edged

Grafting a New Neck. 45

chisel, to remove the wood. The back of the scroll I cut quite straight, continuing the line underneath until it emerges just above the second peg-hole, as indicated by the dotted lines

Fig. 10. Back View of 'Cello Scroll from underneath, showing the Shape of the Graft.

in Fig. 8. The line nearest the peg-holes shows the original sweep of the inside of the scroll, the second dotted line shows the extent to which I remove the wood. When this has been

46 Adjusting and Repairing Violins, &c.

successfully accomplished the most ticklish part of the job has been managed.

The next operation requires great attention to correct measurements and straight and clean cutting. I select a piece of good figured sycamore, which, when measured in the rough, is

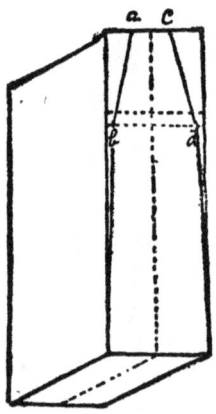

Fig. 11. Method of Setting-out new 'Cello Neck.

14½in. by 5in. by 2½in. The surface (I will afterwards term it the upper surface) which will come in contact with the fingerboard I plane perfectly level and true, testing every portion of it to see that it is as true as it is possible to make it. Down its exact centre I draw a line, continuing this through the lower end, and also

Grafting a New Neck. 47

through the upper end and along the lower surface. This line, in fact, cuts the block of wood clean in two; it must be accurately drawn, as from it all measurements must be made, and on the exactness of these measurements depend the perfect fitting and poise of the neck. The lower end is supposed to be perfectly true. At

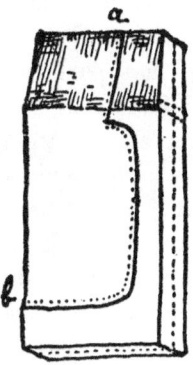

Fig. 12. Side View of new 'Cello Neck.

a distance of 11¼in. I draw a line at perfect right angles to the centre perpendicular, and at the distance of 11½in. another line.

I now proceed to mark off a width at each side of the centre line which corresponds to the width of the interior of the peg-box at the place where the graft should taper away; and at the lower of the two lines, previously marked on the upper surface, I mark off the width of the lower opening of the peg-box (points a, b, c, d, Fig. 11). This wood I remove, first with a saw, then with a little iron plane.

The next thing is to mark roughly the dotted outline, a, b, in Fig. 12, and to remove the wood with the saw, leaving sufficient margin for finer working. After the upper part of the bevelled graft has been planed and smoothed, the scroll should fit exactly that part of the graft which has been prepared for it.

The neck I trim almost to its correct shape. The centre line, which has been obliterated, I once more supply, and this line is kept in evidence until the work is almost complete. The neck is now worked out to something nearing its roundness, and the lower part, or root, which has previously been roughly bevelled, is made to assume more its exact shape.

The Slope of the Neck.

Now comes a most important matter—*i.e.*, the exact poise or slope of the neck. The regular maker has of course a template for the neck, so that the whole thing can be sawn out in the rough, and the exact bevel required at the lower end of the root is previously known. In fitting a new graft to an old 'cello we have

Grafting a New Neck.

not such a guide. The repairer's template, besides giving the height of the bridge, also gives the slope of the fingerboard. We must therefore proceed to construct such a one for our present purpose.

The height of the bridge in this instance is exactly 3¾in. Now, the height at which the neck projects above the belly is ¾in.; to this

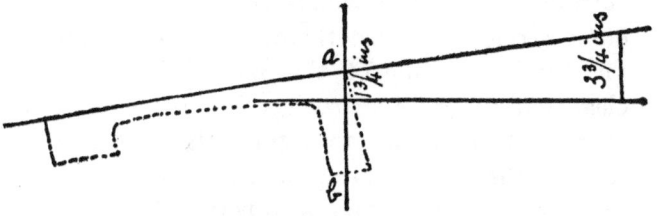

Fig. 13. Diagram showing the Method of Obtaining the correct "Set" of the 'Cello Neck.

I add another ¾in. for the thickness at this point of the fingerboard, and another ¼in. for the space between the strings and the board. Now, the slope of this line will, if it is carried on to the full length of the neck, and due allowance is made for the tapering of the fingerboard, &c., give me the exact set of the neck. The lines *a*, *b*, in Fig. 13, can now be worked out truthfully.

Before absolutely finishing this lower portion

of the graft we must see in what state is the cutting in the upper block. If the edges of the ribs, which fit to the neck, are at all torn or jagged, another cutting must be made; and if they are badly torn a piece of rib must be let in and another groove cut. In this case I find the cutting is as good as new. I also notice something else. The maker, fearful of the neck coming away, has given a good bevel to his cutting, the sides of which slope inwards to the outer surface. I must therefore make allowance for this in finishing off the root of the neck. I clean out the cutting, seeing that the edges are sharp and quite free from glue; then I trim the root of the graft, trying it from time to time to see that I am arriving at a perfect fit.

The root of the neck is now roughly in its correct shape, and I can proceed with the upper end of the graft. The scroll is glued, firmly clamped in position, and allowed ample time for the glue to harden. The wood from the interior of the peg-box is then mortised out, and finished with a fine cutting chisel, and lastly with file and glass-paper. And now is revealed the correctness of this portion of the work; if neatly fitted in the earlier stages, the place where the new wood meets the old is scarcely discernible, and afterwards, when the discolour-

Grafting a New Neck.

ing stain and the varnish are applied, it is quite hidden. The peg-holes are re-bored, first with ordinary brace and bit, then with a tapering bit, and, lastly, finished with a tapering or "rat-tailed" file.

The gluing and clamping of the neck will be dealt with in the next chapter.

CHAPTER VIII.

FIXING THE NECK AND FINGERBOARD.

The neck is now ready to be glued to the body of the 'cello dealt with in the preceding chapters.

Gluing and Clamping the Neck.

The method of clamping the neck in position is illustrated in Fig. 14. The neck should fit in its groove almost air-tight. It is impossible to get any downward pressure from the clamps; the only pressure I can apply is that which forces the neck home, tightly wedging it and causing it to adhere rigidly to the block and the button at the back. The glue which oozes out—and I take care that it *does* ooze out—is now wiped away.

In this operation it **is** essential to be fairly liberal with the glue, as much of it will soak into the new neck; in some cases it may be found necessary to take out the neck and to

Fixing the Neck and Fingerboard.

give another application of glue before applying the clamps. This should be attended to. If, however, the best glue is used, and it is seen to ooze out all along the edges of the root of the neck, we may rest assured that the job has been well done.

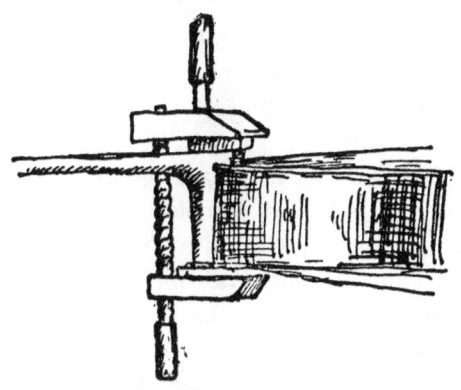

Fig. 14. Method of Clamping the new Neck to the Body of the 'Cello.

Preparing and Gluing the Fingerboard.

The fingerboard is now prepared for gluing in place. Here I would like to utter a word of protest against the thick, ugly fingerboards which one finds on most modern 'cellos. The board may be purchased wholesale or retail ready made; it, however, requires some treatment. I hollow it out on the under-side, and this hollow I continue as far as the root of the neck. I then finish the under-side as carefully and smoothly as if it were on view, and that part which is to come in contact with the neck I test, and see that it is perfectly level and true. It should fit the neck so perfectly that no line is visible. I glue and clamp the fingerboard in the usual way, applying pressure by two clamps, and using a piece of board for the upper-side and two pieces of cork or rubber or paper pads for the neck.

The nut I cut and glue in position, making the cuts for the strings, rounding them off with a file and making as smooth as possible, so that the strings move quite freely along the channels. The distance at which these cuts are made is an important matter. If at too great a distance from each other the strings are difficult to manipulate, whereas if too close the player cannot finger the strings independently. The distance from the centre of each cut or channel is slightly more than ¼in. A quarter of an inch would do, but it is on the near side. The distance apart of the strings at the bridge should be slightly under ¾in.

Wetting before Varnishing.

The graft and the edges of the fingerboard I smooth down with file, scraper, and glass-paper,

Fixing the Neck and Fingerboard.

and as I do it I repeatedly wet the whole surface with water, letting the water soak into the wood, and when dry again going over the surface with fine glass-paper. One professional maker to whom I mentioned this method said, somewhat sarcastically, "You may keep on wetting the surface until doomsday, and it will yet appear rough at the first coat of varnish." Well, that may be true, but it will be found that it will not be so rough as if the wetting process had never been tried.

Staining and Varnishing.

The neck I stain with a vandyke stain, and once more I sand-paper the surface until the figure or curl stands out; then I varnish the whole with spirit varnish. The part of the scroll and also the lower part of the root of the neck I tint as previously explained, in order to bring the white wood to something like the shade of the old wood, and these portions I give four or five coats of good oil-varnish, rubbing down with pumice-powder and finishing with oil and Tripoli powder. Varnishing is, however, such an important matter as to require a chapter for its consideration.

CHAPTER IX.

VARNISHING.

I WILL now give details of my method of varnishing and finishing off the new portions of a repaired violin.

Preparing.

It is essential that the new wood should be perfectly clean and absolutely free from fingermarks. The wood is smoothed by a light rubbing with very fine glass-paper. If after the final application of this there are any signs of the surface of the wood being scratched or torn up, it will be advisable to reduce the abrasive power of the glass-paper by rubbing two pieces together, and then using. Another method is to save for the final papering any used pieces of glass-paper that have had the surface worn almost away.

Even with these aids the amateur repairer may not be able to produce a surface which is absolutely smooth and glistening. Much depends

Varnishing. 57

upon the correct amount of pressure being used, and it is often advisable to glass-paper only *with* the grain. Any attempt to paper across the grain of very soft pine will cause a scratched surface which no amount of subsequent glass-papering will quite remedy.

Moistening.

The surface of the wood should now be moistened with water and allowed to dry. It will be found that not only does the grain of the wood rise, but also that any imperfections in the finishing are more apparent. By alternately wetting the surface and lightly papering when quite dry, a very smooth surface, which will not rough when the varnish is applied, will eventually be arrived at.

Varnish

Every maker and repairer swears by his own varnish, and indeed it is difficult to say whose varnish is the best. I have come to the conclusion that, although a great deal depends upon the quality of the varnish, yet more depends on how it is applied. The same varnish in different makers' hands will in the finished work partake of very different characteristics. As I have had some excellent results from Whitelaw's varnish (which may be obtained from Mr. J. W. Briggs, Cambridge Street, Glasgow), I will confine my instructions to the best method of applying that preparation. The varnish is supplied in two kinds. First, the pale amber varnish, which must be used to give the primary coats. Secondly, the coloured varnish. The latter is slightly thicker than the pale amber, but is sufficiently thin to work quite easily. I also provide myself with a 1in. hog-hair flat—the style of brush which artists use.

Varnishing.

In varnishing the whole of a violin, the following precautions are necessary. The peg-holes should be filled up with corks, which may be cut off quite close to the wood. A long pin of wood may also be fitted in the hole from which the end plug has been taken. This wooden pin is convenient, as the violin can be rested on the pin and easily turned about during the varnishing.

Pour a small quantity of the pale amber varnish into a saucer or other flat vessel. Commence varnishing the ribs. Do not have the brush too fully charged with varnish—just sufficient to flow nicely without either having to "scrub" the varnish or having any fear that it will run in "tears." The back of the violin may next be

Varnishing. 59

treated. Squeeze out the varnish on the highest curves, and work downwards towards the hollows. The scroll is next treated, and finally the belly. The violin should be suspended in such a way that the upper table is in a horizontal position; thus the risk of having " tears " of varnish running out of the sound-holes is avoided.

Several days should elapse before another coat of varnish is applied. It is no good being in a hurry; in fact, it is far better to delay a day or two than to run the risk of spoiling the work. If the coats of varnish are applied too rapidly a brilliant finish is impossible; moreover, the half-hardened undercoats are liable to sweat, causing a mildewed appearance when finished.

As a rule, two or three coats of the pale amber varnish are sufficient. The coloured varnish may then be applied. After giving two coats of the coloured varnish it is advisable to rub off the top skin. This is accomplished by the following method : Powder a piece of rosin (the ordinary plumber's rosin is quite good enough); when it is absolutely certain that the last coat of varnish applied is perfectly set, rub the entire surface with the powdered rosin. Rub with a circular motion, using the thumb or the tips of the fingers. Be careful not to rub a hole in the varnish—that is, do not go below the outer skin. If this has been successfully accomplished the whole surface will be perfectly smooth, but absolutely without shine.

After carefully wiping away the surplus rosin, proceed with the remaining coats of varnish. It is sometimes necessary to give as many as eight coats in all, but I have found that six or seven coats are often sufficient. The last coat is rubbed down as before with powdered rosin, and the final polishing is given with Tripoli powder in the following way :

Polishing.

Make ready two saucers, one containing a good thick soap lather, the other a small quantity of the Tripoli powder. Smear a small piece of flannel with the soap lather, and on this sprinkle the powder. Now rub the whole surface, a small portion at a time, with the powder. Remember that the action of the Tripoli powder is to soften the surface of the varnish, and the soap lather will counteract this tendency. Keep the cloth moving, and if the varnish tends to become at all sticky, apply more soap lather.

The above is the most usual way of finishing off, but many makers use oil instead of soap lather, and some dispense with the Tripoli powder entirely and finish with the oil alone. Another

Varnishing.

way is to finish with the brush—that is, to leave the varnish in its natural state. I do not recommend this, as the surface is too glaring. A medium course may be taken by rubbing down as directed, then, instead of the Tripoli polishing, giving a final coat of varnish thinned down with turps. In all repair work, however, the only method is to give the final polishing with Tripoli powder, for in no other way can the proper mellow appearance be arrived at.

CHAPTER X.

THE SOUND-POST.

THE sound-post, as I have remarked in an earlier chapter, acts as a transmitter of vibrations from the belly to the back, and thus to the air-space; also as a medium for localising the vibrations, and forms what is known as a node or nodal point. Its real character has always been shrouded in mystery, many writers upholding the now exploded theory that the sound-post is merely a support for the bridge. If that were the case it would matter little in which position the post was fitted, so long as it was sufficiently *near* the foot of the bridge. We shall find, however, that the functions of the sound-post are of a far more delicate nature than they would be if it merely acted as a support.

One of the chief functions of the sound-post is to form a node. A node is, perhaps, best described as the axis. It is in reality the one

The Sound-Post. 63

blank spot in the vibrating body. In playing harmonics on the violin or 'cello the harmonic note is formed by lightly touching the string at a given place, thus forming a nodal point. The character of the vibrations is wholly determined by the position of this nodal point, and in many instances the vibrations produced by its formation are totally different in character from those produced by the same length of string vibrating under normal conditions. This applies with equal force to the duties of the sound-post. If the nodal point formed by the sound-post is moved in the slightest degree the whole character of the vibrations is altered.

The sound-post must be of exactly the correct length, and the correct length is that which allows the post just to stand when the tension is taken off the belly. If the post is so long that it is firmly wedged between back and belly it is too long, and the tone will be tense; if it is so short that it falls immediately the bridge is taken down it is too short, and the tone will be dull and thin.

There are several other matters which should be mentioned with respect to the thickness, weight, and density of the sound-post.

The sound-post must not take up too much air-space. Yet it should be of sufficient thickness, and it must contain a sufficient number of "threads" or "grain" to act as a sound-conductor. A thick post of pulpy wood is not of much use. As a rule the post should be slightly thinner than the sound-hole at its centre. If the wood of the sound-post is of too great a density the post will be too heavy and the vibrations will be impeded.

If the repairer has a keen ear he may readily make use of these idiosyncrasies of the sound-post to improve a defective instrument. Thus a violin or violoncello with a "screaming" tone may be fitted with a thick post of soft wood; whereas an instrument of mellow tone may be made more brilliant by the use of a sound-post made of slightly thinner wood, the grain of which is close and well-defined.

CHAPTER XI.

REPAIRING A BULGE IN THE BACK.

THE next instrument I am going to work at is an old Italian violin. It is of beautiful appearance, with lovely orange varnish. The upper table is of pine, of that class which contains beautiful curls, almost like the markings in a piece of wainscoting oak. There is only one very great fault about the construction, which gives the instrument away as being of secondrate origin, otherwise I should not have been surprised to find the name Amati on its ticket. The fault is its back. The back is of a very plain gnarled sort of wood; it scarcely looks like sycamore, but it is sycamore, and not beech. The manufacturer has made one grand mistake : he has made the back too thin, and the character of the wood has accentuated this fault. Directly under the foot of the sound-post is a huge hollow; looking at the back from the outside

66 Adjusting and Repairing Violins, &c.

it appears as a large, bulging lump. It must be our business to set this right.

Removing the Back.

Removing the strings, bridge, tailpiece, &c., I take out the sound-post, and marvel at its length—quite ½in. longer than a violin of this model requires, showing that, as the back bulged, the previous owners, or the repairers to whom the instrument had been entrusted, had supplied a longer post, thus making matters worse. This is an instance where it is compulsory to remove the back. The general rule in effecting repairs to the interior of an instrument is to remove the upper table. I remove the back in a similar manner to that previously explained for taking off the upper table.

Making a Shape to Fit the Hollow.

A slab of sycamore about ½in. thick and 3in. square is now prepared; this I leave with a level and true surface at one side, and the other I cut away with paring chisel and gouge until it is of such a shape that it would have fitted the inside of the back of the violin in its original state. This is not done all in a moment, nor without repeated measuring. During the time occupied by this I apply a

Repairing a Bulge in the Back. 67

poultice of wet rag to the bulge in the back; this I repeat until the fibres of the wood are much softened, and will therefore yield to pressure much more readily than the remainder of the back. I find that the shaping still gives me a thickness of $\frac{1}{4}$in. at the two edges, whereas at the top and bottom and throughout the centre of the little slab of sycamore I have still the original thickness.

Affixing the New Piece.

I now prepare some good strong glue, of the best—not that dark stuff which is all smell and no stick; rapidly glue the surface of the back, and also the bevelled surface of the piece of sycamore, and clamp together. Two clamps prove sufficient. In order to distribute the pressure pretty evenly, I have a square of cork about 1in. thick, large enough to cover the place under treatment, and put this at the outside—the varnished side of the back—while on the inside, against the slab of sycamore, I clamp another slab of sycamore cut from the same piece.

Working-down the New Wood.

After leaving the back for a day, I again take it in hand. Having previously measured the thickness throughout the back with callipers, I am prepared to work the new wood down until there is just sufficient of it left to withstand the pressure of the sound-post. In the old Italian violin I find that it will stand quite a sixteenth of an inch for a space about as large as half-a-crown. I carefully gouge away the wood until I have arrived almost at this thickness, plus the thickness of the back. Then, taking this as a centre, I work out the wood until it gradually tapers down at the edges. I finish off with sand-paper, and so smooth off the edges that it is almost impossible to tell where the original wood of the back leaves off and where the new wood commences.

Finishing.

The new wood I stain with permanganate of potash or with a vandyke stain used for staining violin necks; and after affixing the back to the instrument in the usual way, the repairs are brought to a satisfactory conclusion.

CHAPTER XII.

INSERTING A PIECE IN THE UPPER TABLE.

THERE is yet another class of repair which the amateur repairer or collector of stringed instruments will find frequently necessary; it is the insertion of a piece of wood in the upper table.

The violin which requires this operation is an early Italian of no name; it has, or rather had in its young days, a pale orange varnish. The varnish now has mellowed down considerably, making the introduction of new wood and new varnish a matter of some consideration and not a little artistic skill. The fracture is a very serious one (Fig. 15); it has evidently been caused during the days when violin cases were scarce and baize bags were common, and when it was customary to carry the bow in the bag along with the violin. In my young days I once created a very similar fracture by carelessly

70 Adjusting and Repairing Violins, &c.

pushing the bow into the bag which contained my violin. The wood is so badly broken—some of the pieces are also missing—that it will be impossible to effect the repairs unless a new piece of fairly generous proportions be inserted.

Choice of Wood.

Once more I bring out the remains of the old piano sound-board, and with the greatest care

Fig. 15. Large Fracture in Upper Table of Violin.

select a fragment which has the reed or grain of the pine of exactly similar size. The hard portions or threads correspond exactly, both in thickness and in width from thread to thread.

Direction of Grain in the Upper Table.

I must here explain how the thread or grain runs in the upper table, or belly, of a violin. The upper table is, of course cut out of a flat piece of pine. Fig. 16 shows a section of the

Inserting a Piece in the Upper Table. 71

belly lengthwise, and also how the thread runs quite evenly straight through from end to end.

Now, as far as the surface is concerned, it will readily be understood that at *a* (Fig. 16) we have not the same surface as at *b*, and at *c* it

Fig. 16. Section of Upper Table (lengthwise), showing disposition of grain.

is again different. At *b* the wood runs parallel for a little space with the upper surface of the thread, whereas at *a* and *c* the surface of the upper table cuts through the threads. The piece of pine to be inserted must therefore be cut

Fig. 17. Faulty Method of Inserting New Piece.

from the wood at precisely the same angle as the wood which adjoins the fracture.

If I insert a piece as at *a, b*, in Fig. 17, the result will be quite a different surface to receive the varnish from that which appears at the surrounding portions. No amount of doctoring with stain will then be of any use, and no matter how cleverly the varnish is matched the new piece will shine like a piece of pearl, quite different from that portion of the belly which adjoins it.

Fig. 18 shows a cross section of the upper

Fig. 18. Cross-section of Upper Table.

table; it will be seen that the threads of pine run through it perpendicularly. The piece of new wood must therefore be cut in such a way that the threads correspond in their direction with those of the old wood. Thus, if a piece of

Fig. 19. Faulty Method of Inserting New Piece.

pine were inserted which had been cut from a piece of wood of about the thickness of the upper table, the grain would be as at *a*, *b*, Fig. 19.

Having pointed out where the amateur is likely to err, I will now describe the proper method of inserting the new piece of wood.

Inserting a Piece in the Upper Table.

Preparing the Fracture for the New Piece.

On carefully examining the fracture, I see which portions of the wood can be glued back in place and which should be removed, and eventually decide on making a clean oblong cut, slightly narrower at the upper end.

The upper table is removed in the manner described in a previous chapter, and, once more bringing the mounting-board into use, I prepare to make the incision. The edges I am most particular to cut quite clean and true. The sides of the cut do not give much trouble, but the upper end which cuts across the grain is likely to be troublesome. This difficulty I get over by selecting an exceedingly sharp chisel, and by providing myself with a block of hard wood on which to rest the interior of the belly while making the incision. I cut from the outside—or varnished side—inwards, so that the part which is on view receives the cleanest initial cut, while the only chance of jagged edges is at the interior, and there they can be finished with a sharp, keen-edged knife.

Having once more tested the grain of the new piece to be inserted, I trace on a piece of pasteboard the cutting I have made in the belly, and this I cut out and test as to size. Laying the pattern on the place where the grain corresponds with that of the violin, I trace and cut out the piece to be inserted. This I am careful to see has its sides quite perpendicular, the importance of which will be seen if Fig. 20 is consulted.

Fig. 20. Section of Portion of Upper Table, showing method of inserting new wood. The piece is afterwards trimmed to shape.

The sketch gives a section of the upper table, and shows the method of inserting the new piece. At last I am satisfied that the piece fits to perfection.

Mounting-board for the Upper Table.

I now prepare my mounting-board once more. After gluing the edges of the fracture and carefully putting the piece in place, I put the belly on the mounting-board, and secure it in position by inserting large steel drawing-pins in the mounting-board as indicated in Fig. 21. When the glue is properly set, I proceed to pare down the wood until it corresponds with the outline of the table, and finish it off with glass-paper. One need not be alarmed if one rubs off some of the varnish of the belly: even if it were possible to make the joint without doing so, it would not be advisable, as the glue-line would inevitably

Inserting a Piece in the Upper Table.

show. By smoothing a little of the old surface as well as the new, one gets a unity of surface not otherwise attainable.

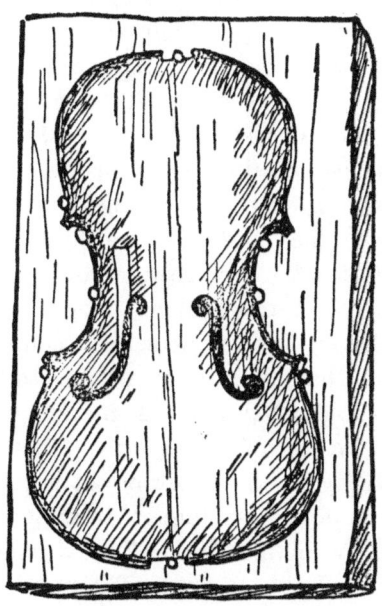

Fig. 21. Method of Obtaining Pressure in Repairing Fractures in Centre of Upper Table. The body is mounted upon a board, and is held by large drawing-pins inserted along its edge.

Colouring and Dull-polishing.

I now add a couple of the small studs to give stability to the repair, and replace the belly. The new wood I wet with luke-warm water, then rub down with fine glass-paper once more. I then rub in a little gamboge stain, and with a camel-hair pencil dipped in vandyke brown (water-colour) colour the wood to match several marks and bruises which have their abrupt termination at the new wood inserted. By so doing I most likely bring down the wrath of many makers who have not had the good sense to bring all the art and device possible to their aid in making their repairs a real part of the original work; but that does not affect me nor mar the result of my efforts. A clever restorer of pictures does not put brilliant new colour upon the work of the old master, but tempers his colours in such a manner that the new colour is scarcely discernible from the old. I merely adopt the same plan in restoring my old Italian violin, which is to my mind a work of art requiring just as careful and as intelligent treatment as the pictures of the old masters. The varnish having been applied, I rub it down with pumice-powder until I obtain the same "dull polish." Having arrived at that point, I am more than proud when my friends say, "I cannot distinguish the new wood from the old."

CHAPTER XIII.

PURFLING.

It is a far more difficult matter to add the purfling to complete a repair than it is to purfle a new instrument. The reason is that in the case of a repair the purfling already in existence has to be accurately matched, and, besides this, the exact curves have to be continued. In many of the old Italian instruments the purfling is exceedingly narrow. In order to match this it is necessary to sand-paper the bought lengths of purfling until the correct width is attained. Even then the centre strip of black wood may be much too broad.

Tracing the Lines.

The purfling is inserted in the following manner. A tool consisting of a couple of adjustable tracers—fine steel points—and a revolving wheel is required. The steel points are so adjusted that they mark two lines exactly the width of the purfling at a given distance from the edge of the violin table. The wood between these two lines has to be removed to, say, half the thickness of the violin belly.

Cutting the Lines.

Here I must caution the amateur against inserting the purfling too deeply. If the steel cutters are allowed to press into the wood too deeply the result will be that the edge of the violin table will be apt to break away.

After the lines have been carefully traced with the purfling tool I take a very fine-edged chisel —a ¾in. joiner's chisel will do for all the big curves, but a smaller one will be needed for the sharp curves at the corners. It is essential that this chisel should have a very keen edge, as scarcely any pressure must be used for it to bite into the wood. Holding the chisel perfectly upright, the lines are accentuated until I find that the proper depth has been arrived at. The wood is then removed from the groove, taking great care that no splinters are caused, which may destroy the line of the purfling.

Bending and Inserting the Purfling.

The next thing to do is to bend a prepared slip of purfling until the required curve is arrived

Purfling.

at. A tool called a bending-iron is used. This tool is formed of a hollow cylinder on a stand, into which a heating-iron can be inserted. The amateur may use an ordinary flat-iron, or any iron that will retain sufficient heat for the purpose. The heating-iron must be hot, and the heat with only a very gentle pressure should accomplish the object. In filling in a short piece of purfling to complete a repair it is advisable to bend a length of purfling twice or thrice the length of the required repair. The portion which exactly fits the groove can then be cut out.

Very little now remains to be done. The groove is brushed over with thin glue, the purfling is pressed into position, and the superfluous glue wiped away with a damp rag. The violin is now put aside until the next day, when, the glue being set, the work is carefully scraped and papered until a smooth surface results.

Conclusion.

In concluding this small volume, I may say that, although the work of repairing and adjusting violins is to me but a hobby, it is one which has been exceedingly useful in my professional career, as if I have had any trouble in getting necessary repairs executed I have quickly solved the difficulty by doing the work myself. It also has been profitable in another direction. I have been able to turn many derelict old violins into instruments of real worth. I trust that my readers will be able to apply the knowledge they may have gained from perusing this manual, and that they also will find that to attempt to repair and restore old instruments is to enlarge one's appreciation of the beauty of the work of the old masters.

INDEX.

A.

Ammonia for cleaning, 13

B.

Back, making shape to fit hollow in, 66
   removing, 66
   repairing bulge in, 65
   varnishing, 58
Bags v. cases, 69
Barley, soaked, for cleaning interior, 33
Bass-bar, 20
   inserting new, 22
   length of, 23
   position of, 22, 24
   removing, 16
Belly or upper table, clamping, 24
   direction of grain in, 70
   gluing, 24
   inserting piece in, 69
   obtaining pressure on, when repairing, 75
   padding, for repair, 17
   preparing, for new piece, 73
   refixing, 24

Belly or upper table, removing, 14
   repairing, 17
   repairing corners of, 18
   repairing large fracture in, 69
   repairs without removing, 32
   sections of, 70-72
   varnishing, 59
Bending-iron, 3
   for purfling, 79
Blotting-paper pads, 18
Bridge, adjusting, 30
   faulty, 5
   fitting, 5
   ill-fitting, 5, 7
   legs and feet of, 7
   trimming, 5
Briggs' varnish, 58
Bulge in back, repairing, 65
Button, ebony rim for, 41
   strengthening and enlarging, 40
Buttons or studs. *See* Studs.

C.

Church instruments of old, 31
Clamps, 3, 24

Cleaning, 13
  ammonia for, 13
  interior, 33
  soaked barley for, 33
  spirits for, 13
Closing fractures without removing belly, 34, 36, 37
  fractures with thread and button, 34, 36
Colouring, 27, 68, 75, 76
  new wood, 55
Corners of belly, repairing, 18
Cotton-rag, removing, 33
Cracks, mending, 11, 17, 31, 34, 69
Cramps, 3, 24

D.

Damping bulge in back, 66
  wood before varnishing, 54, 57, 75
Dull-polishing, 76
Dust, removing, from interior, 33

E.

Eau de Cologne for cleaning, 13
Ebony rim, to strengthen button, 41

F.

Finger-board, gluing, 52
  preparing, 53
Fractures, mending, 11, 17, 31, 34, 69
  mending, without removing belly, 34, 36, 37
Fractures, mending, without removing belly, 34, 36, 37

G.

Glass-papering, 54, 56, 76
Glue, 34
  removing, 13, 15, 33
  softening, 14, 16
Gluing, principles of, 34
Grafting new neck, 42
Grain, direction of, 70

H.

Heaton, Mr. W., 26

I.

Implements used in repairing, 2
Interior, cleaning, 33

M.

Materials, 3, 19, 22, 46, 64, 66, 70
Mirror for sound-post setting, 9
Moistening bulge in back, 66
  wood before varnishing, 54, 57, 75
Mounting-board for belly, 17, 73, 74

N.

Nail through upper block to root of neck, 40
Neck, 52
  clamping, 52
  correct set of, 49
  cutting, 44
  fit of, 53
  grafting, 42
  poise or slope of, 48

Index.

Neck, removing, 39
  root of, 50
  setting-out, 44
  template for, 48, 49
  trimming, 48
New fractures, repairing, without removing belly, 34, 36, 37
  wood, preparing for varnishing, 26
  wood, working down, 67
Node or nodal point, 29, 62
Nut, cutting and gluing, 54

P.

Pad or mounting-board for belly, 17, 73, 74
Padding belly for repair, 17
Pads, blotting-paper, &c., 18, 24
Palette-knife, 16, 25
Peg-box, graft in, 43
Peg-holes, filling, before varnishing, 58
  re-boring, 51
Piano sounding-board wood, 19, 70
Planes, 3
Plug-hole, filling, before varnishing, 58
Polishing, dull, 76
  with Tripoli powder, 60
Purfling, 77
  bending, 78
  cutting lines for, 78
  filling-in short pieces of, 79
  inserting, 78
  tools, 3, 77
  tracing lines for, 77

R.

Register, improving different parts of, 29

Removing back, 66
  bass-bar, 16
  belly, 14
  glue, 13, 15, 33
  neck, 39
  scroll, 44
Ribs, closing fractures in, 34
  drilling holes through, for threads, 35, 36
  repairing, 31
  varnishing, 58
Rosin, rubbing varnish with, 59

S.

Screw-nail through upper block to root of neck, 40
Scroll, gluing, 50
  grafted, 43, 45
  importance of, 42
  lining, with new neck, 43
  removing, 44
  sweep of, 45
  varnishing, 59
Setting-out neck, 44
Smoothing, 54, 56, 76
Sound-post, 62
  cutting, 28
  effects of, on tone, 64
  fit of, 10
  fitting, 9, 28
  functions of, 29, 62
  grain of, 64
  importance of, 30
  length of, 63
  marking position of, 29
  position of, 10, 29
  repairing bulge under, 65
  setter, 9
  thickness of, 28, 63
Spirits for cleaning, caution regarding, 13
Staining, 55, 68, 75, 76
  new wood, 55

Index.

Strings, 'cello, distance of, from fingerboard, 6
  distance of, apart, 6, 54
Studs, 15
  affixing, 20
  buttons, and thread, closing fractures with, 34, 36
  inserting, without removing belly, 37
  number of, 15, 24, 87

T.

Template for neck, 48, 49
Thread and button, closing fractures with, 34, 36
  of wood, fitting, 19
Tinting, 68, 75, 76
  new wood, 55
Tools, 2
  purfling, 77
  special, 3
Tracing lines for purfling, 77
Tripoli powder, polishing with, 60

U.

Upper table. *See* Belly.

V.

Varnish, 27, 57
  Briggs', 58
  coloured, 59
  number of coats of, 59, 60
  pale, 59
  rubbing-off top skin of, 59
  Whitelaw's, 57
Varnishing, 56
  order of procedure, 58
  preparing for, 26, 55, 56
  preparing new wood for, 26
  wetting wood before, 54, 57, 75

W.

Warehouse instruments, repairing, 2
Wetting bulge in back, 66
  wood before varnishing, 54, 57, 75
Whitelaw's violin varnish, 27, 57
Wolf notes, 8, 10
Wood, preparing new, for varnishing, 26
  working down new, 67

Printed in Great Britain by Jarrold & Sons, Ltd., Norwich

www.ingramcontent.com/pod-product-compliance
Lightning Source LLC
Chambersburg PA
CBHW020809160426
43192CB00006B/496